Voyage

Teaching Guide 2

Written by Ann Webley

Contents

OXFORD
UNIVERSITY PRESS

Voyage 2 at a glance

This chart shows you how the stories in Voyage 2 fit with National Curriculum levels and with the requirements of the UK curricula. To help with your planning, it also shows links to the NLS medium-term plans, and summarises the main reading skills covered in the teaching notes on each story.

Story/author	Voyage Level	Approx NC Level	Genre	Link to Medium-term Plans	Reading skills
The Grey Gander: *Chris Buckton*	Lower ✓	2b	Historical story – Tudors	Y4 Term 1 – Narrative: character and setting	Analyse structure/ characterisation; prediction; response
Wave-Eater: *Geraldine McCaughrean*	Upper ✓	3b	Historical story – Vikings	Y4 Term 1 – Narrative: character and setting	Analyse structure/ characterisation; prediction; response
My Name is Jim: *Elaine Canham*	Lower ✓	2b	Historical story – World War 2	Y4 Term 1 – Narrative: character and setting	Analyse structure/ characterisation; prediction; inference; response
A Curse on Yesterday: *Sally Prue*	Upper ✓	3b	Historical story – Romans	Y4 Term 1 – Narrative: character and setting	Analyse structure/ theme/ characterisation; prediction; response
Ubble in Trouble: *Douglas Hill*	Lower ✓	2a	Stories of imagined worlds/ science fiction	Y4 Term 2 – Narrative: setting	Analyse genre features/ setting/ character; response
Monsters: *Douglas Hill*	Upper ✓	3b–3a	Stories of imagined worlds/ science fiction	Y4 Term 2 – Narrative: setting	Analyse genre features/ setting/ character; response
Food for Thought: *Michael Pryor*	Lower ✓	2a	Fantasy adventure	Y4 Term 2 – Narrative: setting	Analyse genre features/ setting/ humour; inference; response
The Boy Who Made Things Up: *Margaret Mahy*	Upper ✓	3b–3a	Fantasy adventure	Y4 Term 2 – Narrative: setting	Analyse genre features/ setting/ characterisation; inference; response
How to Win at Football: *Rachel Anderson*	Lower ✓	3c	Stories that raise issues	Y4 Term 3 – Issues and dilemmas 1	Analyse plot/ paragraphing/ characters; inference; response
Doppelganger.com: *Jan-Andrew Henderson*	Upper ✓	3a	Stories that raise issues	Y4 Term 3 – Issues and dilemmas 1	Analyse plot/ paragraphing/ characters; inference; response
The Rock: *Julie Till*	Lower ✓	3c	Stories from other cultures	Y4 Term 3 – Narrative reading and writing	Analyse setting/ plot; inference; response
Zanzibar Treasures: *Adam Guillain*	Upper ✓	3a	Stories from other cultures	Y4 Term 3 – Narrative reading and writing	Analyse setting/ plot; inference; response

Key NLS objectives	Northern Ireland curriculum	Scottish 5–14 Guidelines for English
Y4T1 T1: settings and characters **Y4T1 T2**: characteristics of key characters **Y4T1 T4**: explore narrative order **Y4T1 T12**: write independently, linked to historical stories	Level 2	Reading for enjoyment: Level B/C Writer's ideas and craft: Level B/C
Y4T1 T1: settings and characters **Y4T1 T2**: characteristics of key characters **Y4T1 T4**: explore narrative order **Y4T1 T12**: write independently, linked to historical stories	Level 3	Reading for enjoyment: Level B/C Writer's ideas and craft: Level B/C
Y4T1 T1: settings and characters **Y4T1 T2**: characteristics of key characters **Y4T1 T3**: explore chronology in narrative **Y4T1 T11**: write character sketches	Level 2	Reading for enjoyment: Level B/C Writer's ideas and craft: Level B/C
Y4T1 T1: settings and characters **Y4T1 T2**: characteristics of key characters **Y4T1 T3**: explore chronology in narrative **Y4T1 T11**: write character sketches	Level 3	Reading for enjoyment: Level B/C Writer's ideas and craft: Level B/C
Y4T2 T1: how writers create imaginary worlds **Y4T2 T3**: compare and contrast settings **Y4T2 T4**: well-chosen words and phrases **Y4T2 T10**: use of settings in own writing.	Level 2	Reading for enjoyment: Level B/C Writer's ideas and craft: Level B/C Awareness of genre: Level B/C
Y4T2 T1: how writers create imaginary worlds **Y4T2 T3**: compare and contrast settings **Y4T2 T4**: well-chosen words and phrases **Y4T2 T10**: use of settings in own writing.	Level 3	Reading for enjoyment: Level C Writer's ideas and craft: Level C Awareness of genre: Level C
Y4T2 T1: how writers create imaginary worlds **Y4T2 T3**: compare and contrast settings **Y4T2 T4**: expressive and descriptive language **Y4T2 T13**: own examples of descriptive and expressive language	Level 2	Reading for enjoyment: Level B/C Writer's ideas and craft: Level B/C Awareness of genre: Level B/C
Y4T2 T1: how writers create imaginary worlds **Y4T2 T3**: compare and contrast settings **Y4T2 T4**: expressive and descriptive language **Y4T2 T13**: own examples of descriptive and expressive language	Level 3	Reading for enjoyment: Level C Writer's ideas and craft: Level C Awareness of genre: Level C
Y4T3 T1: social, cultural and moral issues **Y4T3 T3**: how paragraphs are used **Y4T3 T11**: write a story about a dilemma	Level 2	Reading for enjoyment: Level B/C Writer's ideas and craft: Level B/C
Y4T3 T1: social, cultural and moral issues **Y4T3 T3**: how paragraphs are used **Y4T3 T11**: write a story about a dilemma	Level 3	Reading for enjoyment: Level C Writer's ideas and craft: Level C
Y4T3 T1: social, cultural and moral issues **Y4T3 T2**: focus on e.g. differences in place, time, customs, relationships **Y4T3 T12**: write alternative ending for known story.	Level 2	Reading for enjoyment: Level B/C Writer's ideas and craft: Level B/C Awareness of genre: Level B/C
Y4T3 T1: social, cultural and moral issues **Y4T3 T2**: focus on e.g. differences in place, time, customs, relationships **Y4T3 T12**: write alternative ending for known story.	Level 3	Reading for enjoyment: Level C Writer's ideas and craft: Level C Awareness of genre: Level C

Voyage and Assessment for Learning

Assessment for Learning is:

"…the process of seeking and interpreting evidence for use by learners and their teachers to decide where the learners are in their learning, where they need to go and how best to get there." (Assessment Reform Group)

In recent years, there has been plenty of research into the ways in which effective assessment can help improve children's learning. As a result, teachers are now being encouraged to apply Assessment for Learning principles to their work with even the youngest pupils. Assessment for Learning is a continuous process, with assessment feeding into planning for future teaching and learning.

In a nutshell, Assessment for Learning involves:

◆ sharing learning intentions/objectives and success criteria with pupils
◆ giving oral and written feedback to pupils based on these intentions/objectives, with the feedback relating directly to pupils' learning in a way that they can understand and act upon
◆ the use of questioning to help pupils express and discuss their ideas and their understanding
◆ the nurturing of pupils as independent learners through the development of self assessment and peer assessment.

These principles can sound rather dry and abstract out of context, but once in use they can be an incredibly powerful force for improvement. The Voyage teaching notes contain elements that will help you to build Assessment for Learning approaches into your guided reading sessions:

◆ a box at the start of each set of notes which puts the learning objectives for each session into child-friendly language
◆ use of questioning at key points throughout each session
◆ a 'Summing up' section at the end of the notes on each story, which helps children sum up what they feel they have learned – in terms both of knowledge and of reading skills and strategies.

In addition, the photocopy master on page 5 can be customised for use after children have read any of the Voyage stories, by adding the story title and the learning objectives for each session at the top. The chart gives children a format within which to express their views on the story and say which objectives they feel most confident about as a result of the session. There is also a chance for them to identify areas of learning with which they feel they need more help. This can help you to plan their next steps.

If children find it difficult to sum up what they have learned in a session, or if they are unable to describe areas of difficulty, it may be worth spending more time discussing the learning objectives for each session with the children, both at the start and at the end of a session.

Self assessment form

Name _____ Date _____

Story title:

Our objectives when we were reading this story were:

What did you think of the story? Did you enjoy it, or not? Give your reasons.	
Look at the objectives listed above this chart. Write down the ones you feel you understand best. Be prepared to explain to someone else what you learned about these objectives!	
Is there anything you didn't understand, or anything you'd like to work on some more? Write it here.	

The Grey Gander
by Chris Buckton

Year 4 Term 1 Historical stories (Tudor)

Teaching objectives

◆ Y4T1 T1 investigate settings and characters (both sessions)
◆ Y4T1 T2 main characteristics of key characters (Session 2)
◆ Y4T1 T4 explore narrative order; map out main stages of a story (Session 1)
◆ Y4T1 T12 write independently, linking own experience to situations in historical stories (Session 2)

NC level 2B

In session 1 We are going to:
◆ look at the main stages in the story
◆ discuss how we know when this story was set.

In session 2 We are going to:
◆ look more carefully at words to describe setting
◆ find out more about Wat through drama.

Quick check
Things to note about this story:
◆ development of the plot
◆ evidence of historical setting
◆ detail of setting
◆ Wat's character and changes of feeling

Session 1: Reading the text

Story introduction

Explain the purpose of the session: *'We are going to read a story, look at the main stages of the plot and talk about when the story was set.'*

Read the first four paragraphs to the children, to 'He was in too much of a hurry to get out of the rain'. Ask the children what they think the story will be about. (Do they pick up the clue about the latch being left undone?) Ask the children if the story is set today. How do they know? *(Old-fashioned name for the boy, working for a Lord of the Manor, making medicines from plants, emptying the privy, geese grazing on village green.)* Check understanding of 'privy' and 'gander'.

Strategy check

Remind the children to pay attention to commas when reading aloud. Model reading a paragraph containing several commas if necessary.

Remind children to break down unfamiliar words into syllables.

Independent reading

If you wish to check children's reading aloud, ask them to take turns and read aloud as far as 'At least he could use them to tip his arrows' (page 4). Alternatively they could each read this passage silently.

Ask them to comment as they read about anything that tells us the story is set in the past. *(Mention of a 'watchman', rubbing fat on chest to keep out cold, people's attitude to the Lord, use of arrows.)*

Pause

Ask the children to discuss what they think Wat will do. How will he be feeling? Look for evidence in the text. *(Importance of the gander, probably no Christmas dinner.)*

Ask the children to read to the end of the story, either independently or aloud in the group.

Returning and responding to the text

Were the children's predictions right? Did they think Wat would get into trouble or did they think he would do something to put the mistake right?

Ask the children to help you plot the storyline on a large sheet of paper or whiteboard. Help them to skim the story to identify the main parts of the plot. Ask the children when they think this story was set and why they think that. *(The author describes it as a story set in Tudor times but many children will say more generally the Middle Ages. This is perfectly correct given the evidence. Rural life remained almost unchanged for hundreds of years.)*

Before the next session

Reread the story and ask the children to make some notes about what they know about Wat, ready for a drama activity.

Session 2: Going deeper

Story introduction – recap

Ask the children to retell the story quickly around the group. They should listen carefully to each other so they can carry on with the narrative when it is their turn.

Independent reading

Explain that short stories have to build up detail about settings very quickly. Last session was about the time the story was set. This time, ask the children to reread and look carefully at the words and phrases that build up setting. (It may be appropriate to ask them to reread only a section – for example the annotated section below, from page 4.)

Returning and responding to the text

Share your own response to particular words and phrases and discuss those that the children noticed. Discuss how the words and phrases help to build up a picture in the reader's mind of the area where Wat's family lives.

Detail of gate – links back to being left open earlier in story.

Mention of mud – helps reader to picture the pen.

Tells reader in detail where the other two geese are – we can picture it.

> But in the morning there was a terrible sight. The gate swung loose, and there were feathers and blood in the mud. The two geese were huddled together at the end of the pen. The gander had gone.
>
> Wat noticed a trail through the mud towards the wood behind their cottage. The fox must have dragged the gander that way. If he could find it, they could still eat it for Christmas.
>
> The trail ended by an old tree. He could see the foxes' den under its roots. There were more feathers and blood, but no gander.

The reader seems to be seeing this as Wat does and gets detail of more mud and the fact that there is a wood behind the cottage. Picture of setting is built up further.

The picture continues – a tree and a den under the roots.

Whole scene is clearly described with simple but well-chosen vocabulary.

Discuss the fact that we know a lot about Wat from the way he reacts and behaves. Establish his feelings at the beginning of the story *(fed up and miserable)*; when he realises the gander has gone *(worried)*; at the end *(relieved)*. Refer back to the text to ensure the children know how to extract this from the story.

Ask the children to take on the role of Wat and talk in more detail about the events of the two days. The teacher should ask questions as necessary to draw out the reasons why he behaved as he did or felt as he did.

Consider the final sentence of the story: 'Wat and his father shared a silent, nervous smile'. Does the role-play show an understanding of the reason for this? *(For example, that Wat and his father are smiling because they are relieved they have escaped being punished, but nervous because they know they are completely dependent on the Lord's good will.)*

If you have time …

Ask the children to look back at the section when Wat is woken in the night. What does he assume when he hears the honking? *(That the gander is keeping the fox away.)* Why does he think that? *(His father has described the gander as 'our watchman'.)* How does this affect the story? *(He thinks nothing is happening – but the reader might wonder because of the clue about the gate.)*

Summing up

Ask the children how the author has helped us picture the setting and understand how Wat feels. *(Setting: use of detail from the past, well chosen words and phrases. How Wat feels – we can tell from how he behaves.)*

Next steps: Independent follow-up

The children could write a short account of when they have done something wrong (like Wat) and what they did about it. Did everything turn out well in the end?

Children could use the photocopiable writing frame on page 54 to help them write a story with a similar structure to *The Grey Gander*.

Wave-Eater

by Geraldine McCaughrean

Year 4 Term 1 Historical stories (Viking)

Teaching objectives

◆ Y4T1 T1 investigate settings and characters (both sessions)

◆ Y4T1 T2 main characteristics of key characters (Session 1)

◆ Y4T1 T4 explore narrative order: map out main stages of a story (Session 1)

◆ Y4T1 T12 write independently, linking own experience to situations in historical stories (Session 2)

NC level 3B

In session 1 We are going to:
- ◆ look at the structure of the story
- ◆ discuss what we know about the main character.

In session 2 We are going to:
- ◆ look at how the author helps the reader to see the scene as the girl experiences it.

Quick check
Things to note about this story:
- ◆ Use of flashback
- ◆ Build-up of setting
- ◆ Change of mood of the main character

Session 1: Reading the text

Story introduction

Explain the purpose of the session: *'We are going to read a story based on a Viking legend and look at the story structure and the main character.'* Read the author's introduction aloud. Ensure that the children know who the Vikings were – a warlike, seafaring race from Scandinavia who were around at about the same time as the Saxons and Normans.

Read aloud the opening paragraph and ask the children what they think is happening. Do not confirm or deny at this stage.

This is a challenging story and it may be a good idea to read the story aloud (in sections) before the children read independently, introducing any vocabulary which may be unfamiliar, e.g. *tyrant, wake.*

Strategy check

Remind children that if they come across unfamiliar words, they should try to work out the meaning from the context but note it down to check later. Remind them to break down unfamiliar words into syllables.

Independent reading

Ask the children to read the next five paragraphs noting the main points of the plot in their reading journal. *(Storm at sea, land spotted, narrator jumps overboard, boat goes on.)* Ask them also to note down in their journals what they find out about the narrator of the story.

Pause

Collect the children's ideas about the main parts of the plot.

Discuss what we know about the narrator so far. Male/female? Adult/child? How does he/she feel? Ask the children to quote evidence from the text.

Ask the children what they think will happen next.

Now ask the children to read to the end of the story.

After reading, ask the children to skim the text and jot down anything they notice about the narrator's mood.

Returning and responding to the text

Look more closely at the structure. Return to the first paragraph and ask the children where it fits in to the story. *(It links with the point where the present-time action picks up again at the top of page 10. A clue to this is the use of the marks on the page between time-changes.)* Discuss the title. *(The Vikings meant that they would conquer the waves with their boat, but here the waves were defeating them.)*

Look at the beginning of the second paragraph – what is it? *(flashback)* and which words in the sentence tell the reader? *(a month ago)*. Discuss why it was a good idea to start with the action in the water *(plunges into action)*.

Map out the events of the story chronologically on a whiteboard or flip-chart. Compare their order to the order in which we read about them.

Ask the children when the reader discovers who the main character is. Do they like the fact that they did not really know? Does it matter? How did the girl's feelings change during the story? *(From scared to confident.)*

If there is time, put one of the group in the "hot-seat" as the girl to explore her feelings at different points of the story.

Before the next session

Ask the children to reread the story. In their reading journals they can draw two 'think' bubbles. They should show what the girl is thinking:

◆ just before she jumps into the water
◆ while she waits on the sand.

Session 2: Going deeper

Story introduction – recap

Share some of the thoughts in the bubbles. (See 'Before the next session'.)

Use this to recap the story briefly.

Independent reading

In this story the setting is built up with carefully chosen words and phrases. Ask the children to read the whole story again, looking out for words and phrases which build up detail about the ship in the storm; and the kind of words the author chooses after the girl sees the doorpost.

Returning and responding to the text

Share ideas with the children and discuss the powerful images for the storm – note that the word 'storm' is not used. The reader infers it from the vocabulary chosen.

Girl's comment to reader – she is there.

Powerful verbs. 'Pit of dark' suggests everything is very serious.

> Floki sent my little brother up the mast, as a look-out. I don't know how he hung on. Wave-Eater would plunge down into a pit of dark, then pitch upwards again. The animals were on their knees, sliding about, boneless with sea-sickness. It took three men on the steering-oar to hold us steady. My mother and aunt climbed into their bed for warmth. Then everything happened at once.

Detailed image of the suffering of the animals.

Detail of part of ship to make the setting very clear.

Last sentence – short sentence starting with 'then' suggests everything is bad but there is worse to come!

Ask the children what they notice about the kind of words used at the beginning and end of the text. Discuss how the choice of words matches the girl's feelings. *(Powerful/sharp images: monstrous waves, plunge, chewing, gripping etc. = fear; 'softer' words: comes nudging and prodding alongside, reaches out, steam, warm = happier, more confident.)* In this way, the reader experiences the feelings with the girl.

Ask the children why they think the Vikings took the doorposts – what might these mean to them? *(Perhaps the end of one part of life and the start of another – out and in. So the girl, sitting between the doorposts, is starting her new life.)*

If you have time …

Point out that some objects seem to have a life of their own. This is another way in which the reader sees the scene as the girl does. *('But a huge wave suddenly <u>pulled itself up</u>'; 'Its partner <u>came nudging and prodding</u> alongside')*

Summing up

Ask the children what they have learned about ways to structure stories and how to bring the setting to life. *(For example, using a flashback so that the story starts at an exciting point; using small details to build up setting with well-chosen words, including powerful verbs)*

Next steps: Independent follow-up

Ask the children to write about a time when they were separated from family or friends, even if this was only for a few minutes. What happened? How did they feel?

Alternatively, they could write about a real or imaginary situation where they had to battle against the elements.

My Name is Jim
by Elaine Canham

. . . .

Year 4 Term 1 Historical stories (World War 2)

Teaching objectives

◆ Y4T1 T1 investigate settings and characters (both sessions)

◆ Y4T1 T2 main characteristics of key characters (Session 2)

◆ Y4T1 T3 explore chronology in narrative (Session 1)

◆ Y4T1 T11 write character sketches (Session 2)

NC level 2B

. . . .

In session 1 We are going to:

◆ look at the main stages in the story

◆ discuss how we know when this story was set.

In session 2 We are going to:

◆ look at how we find out about a character

◆ explore the characters of the two boys through drama.

Quick check

Things to note about this story:

◆ Plot structure – delayed start for story

◆ Evidence of historical setting

◆ Relationship between boys – will it change?

Session 1: Reading the text

Story introduction

Explain the purpose of the session: *'We are going to read a story and look at the main stages of the plot and talk about when the story was set.'*

Read the first three paragraphs to the children, to 'That's what happened in those days'. Ask the children when they think the story is set. *(Mention of war, German buzz bombs, doodlebugs, Germans as the enemy.)* How do they know Jim is talking about the past? *('That's what happened in those days'.)* Establish that we do not know how many years have gone by.

Strategy check

Remind the children to pay attention to commas when reading aloud. (Model reading, if necessary.) Remind children to break down unfamiliar words into syllables.

Independent reading

If you wish to check children's reading aloud, ask them to take turns and read aloud as far as 'He looked really stupid'. Alternatively they could each read this passage silently.

As they read, they should notice other examples that show when the story is set. *(Ted's dad killed; people sent to jail for objecting to war; bombs falling on London; children evacuated; gas masks; air raid sirens; shelters.)*

Pause

Ask the children what they think will happen next. Do they realise the comment at the start ('I want to tell you about the day Ted Baker and I nearly got killed by a German buzz bomb') tells us that Ted will *not* be killed? In this story, the reader knows what the story will be about in the second sentence.

Ask the children to read to the end of the story, either independently or in pairs. Make sure they can read the longer sentence – 'I pushed him off the road…' – clearly.

Returning and responding to the text

Were the children's predictions right? Did they think Jim would save Ted?

Ask the children to help you plot the storyline, using a large sheet of paper or whiteboard. *(Introduction from Jim; what a doodlebug was; relationship between Jim and Ted; incident starts: noise; people run, Ted stays still; Jim saves Ted; effect of bomb; ending – Ted brings banana.)*

Discuss the end of the story. Can the children find the previous reference to bananas? What does this action by Ted show? *(He is trying to make friends, and perhaps to thank Jim, by offering something so scarce.)*

Before the next session

Ask the children to reread the story. Ask half of them to note down in their reading journals what Jim is like and the other half what Ted is like. They will be using their notes in a role-play activity.

Session 2: Going deeper

Story introduction – recap

Ask the children to retell the story of the day Jim saved Ted. Ensure that they understand they are simply recounting from the start of the incident rather than from Jim's introduction to the story.

Independent reading

Explain that short stories need to include lots of detail about what the characters are like, and they do this in many ways. Ask the children to reread the story and note in their reading journals how we know what Jim and Ted are like. It may be necessary to give them an example before they start reading. (*See the annotated text below for ideas.*)

Returning and responding to the text

Share the children's ideas. Question them in order to elicit examples related to (i) what characters say and how they say it; (ii) what characters do; (iii) how characters react; (iv) how others react to them. Ensure they can find evidence in the text to back up what they say.

Information about Jim's feelings.

A lot of things Ted does to Jim – show that Ted is being a bully and is picking on him.

Jim's reaction. Tries to escape but Ted always wins.

Shows Ted is angry.

> I wanted to be sent away. I wanted to get away from Ted. When I went down the road past his mum's shop to school, he would be waiting. He would call me names or take my gas mask. We all had to carry masks, in case the Germans dropped gas bombs on us, but they never did.
>
> Other times he would push me over and rub my face in the dirt. Sometimes I ran away. But he always got me in the end.
>
> Once he grabbed me and shook me until my teeth rattled. "That's for my dad, you little rat," he shouted. "That's for my dad!" And he kept on until his mum came out of the shop and stopped him. She put her arm round him and took him inside.

Shows why Ted hates Jim. He is picking on Jim because Jim's dad refused to fight, and Ted's dad was killed in action.

Ted's mother understands what he was doing. She stopped him but she's not cross.

Half the group should play the part of Jim and the other should play Ted. The 'boys' should talk to each other about the way they feel at different times in the story, for example: at the start, after Ted's father has been killed; when the bomb fell; after Jim saved Ted; after school that day.

Ask the children to come out of role and discuss whether they think the boys will now be friends or go back to how they were. What was Jim expecting and why? (*He expected Ted to carry on as normal so he told him to* go away.) What about Ted? *(He's trying to make friends so he brought the banana.)* Do the children think Jim will be Ted's friend? What would they do in that situation?

If you have time …

Ask the children how the story would have been affected if it had started at paragraph 10 – 'This morning …'. *(Reader wouldn't have understood about doodlebugs or realised Jim and Ted were enemies.)* In this story, the introduction is important to set the scene and let the reader know about characters. In most stories, we find these things out as the story moves along.

Summing up

Ask the children for four ways that an author can give detail about a character. *(What he says and how he says it; what he does; how he reacts; how others react to him.)*

Next steps: Independent follow-up

Ask the children to imagine they are Ted telling someone about the day of the bomb. They could start like this:

Anyway, this morning I had just turned into the street and I saw stupid Jim.

Alternatively, children could use the photocopiable writing frame on page 54 to help them write a story with a similar structure to *My Name is Jim*.

A Curse on Yesterday
by Sally Prue

Year 4 Term 1 Historical stories (Romans)

Teaching objectives

- Y4T1 T1 investigate settings and characters (both sessions)
- Y4T1 T2 main characteristics of key characters (Session 2)
- Y4T1 T3 explore chronology in narrative (Session 1)
- Y4T1 T11 write character sketches (Session 2)

NC level 3B

In session 1 We are going to:
- look at how the setting is built up
- think about the structure of the story.

In session 2 We are going to:
- look at how the author tells us about Cara
- think about the theme behind the story.

Quick check

Things to note about this story:
- Build-up of setting and importance of Sul's grove
- Small gap in chronology
- How Cara's feelings change through the story

Session 1: Reading the text

Story introduction

Explain the purpose of the session: *'We are going to look at the structure of the story and how the setting is built up gradually.'*

Read the opening to the children (to 'with a splintering screech') and ask them what kind of story it is. What genre clues are there? *(Mention of Romans, chariots, goddess Sul, sacred oak.)*

Strategy check

Remind children that if they come across any unfamiliar words as they read, they should try to work out the meaning from the context but note them down to check later.

Remind children to break down unfamiliar words into syllables.

Independent reading

Ask the children to read the next section, up to ' "Send a message to the goddess for me" ', and note down in their journals their immediate responses. Why is Cara upset? Do they think Marbod will help?

Pause

Share the children's reactions. Ensure that they base an opinion on evidence from the text.

Quickly jot down the chronology of the story so far. *(Cara tries to stop axemen, she argues with Marbod.)* Ask the children what they think will happen.

Now tell the children to read to the end of the story.

Returning and responding to the text

Jot down the rest of the plan. *(Marbod writes a curse – but won't give it himself, Cara speaks to goddess, chooses not to curse Romans, meets father – he's working with Romans.)*

Look at the end of the first section that the children read and the beginning of the second. Ask the children if the second section follows straight on in time from the first. They should spot that there is a small gap. Discuss the reason for this. *(To focus on the talk with the goddess which is most important.)*

Ask the children to find examples of the build-up of detail about the setting. *(Gushed hot water, power and bad eggs, steam, bubbles.)* Explain that the smell is sulphur. A powerful image is built up using the senses.

Discuss evidence of the importance of Sul's grove and point out that the reader discovers all this gradually. *(Evidence includes the way both characters feel about it, mention of sacred oaks, voice of the goddess being heard, Cara fleeing 'back to the world of the Romans' – showing that the grove is special.)* Ask the children what is implied when Marbod says, "What shall I tell Sul?" *(For example, even though the Romans have promised him a lot, his religion is very important to him and he is still in awe of the goddess.)* Discuss what all this shows about Sul's grove, and the characters' attitudes to it.

Before the next session

Ask the children to reread the story. Tell half the group to concentrate especially on Cara and the other half on Marbod in order to prepare for a role-play activity next session. They should think about their character's feelings and actions, and how these change through the story.

Session 2: Going deeper

Story introduction – recap

Ask the children to retell the story in a group, taking it in turns to speak. Focus on careful listening so that a child is ready to start from the exact point another finishes.

Independent reading

Explain that in a good short story, the reader very quickly gets to know about the characters. Ask the children to read the story again and note down how the author does this.

Returning and responding to the text

Share the children's ideas and draw out through questioning the idea that we learn about characters through what they say, what they do and how they respond to others. Find examples in the text to illustrate these points. The example below shows how we learn about Cara and her mood from a short passage of text.

Anger in speech verb.

Angry reaction to the axeman. Action and speech. Use of italics for emphasis.

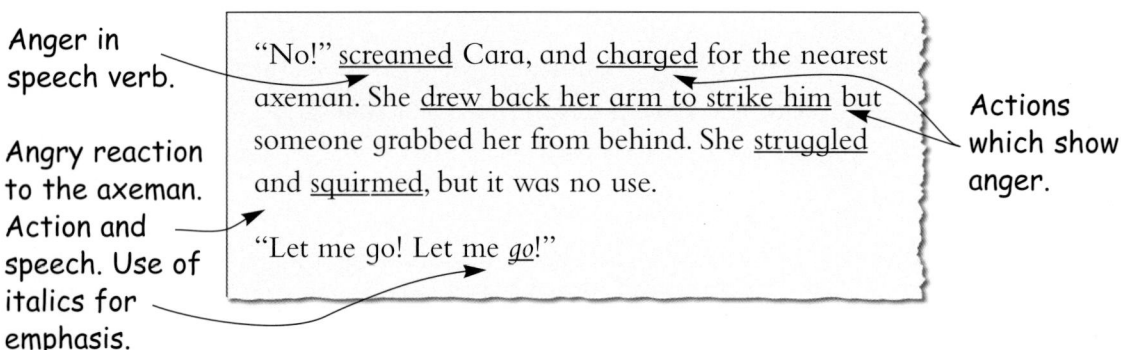

"No!" screamed Cara, and charged for the nearest axeman. She drew back her arm to strike him but someone grabbed her from behind. She struggled and squirmed, but it was no use.

"Let me go! Let me go!"

Actions which show anger.

Set up a role-play activity with half the children playing Cara and the other half playing Marbod. Ask them to role-play the scene a) before they went to the grove; b) when they got there.

Characters are often changed by events. Ask the children if they think Cara will be different at the end of the story. *(She has accepted it was right not to put the curse on the Romans but she is not happy.)*

Ask the children how they think they would feel in Cara's situation. Can they understand why she is not happy with the changes brought by the Romans? How has life changed for other characters in the story since the Romans' arrival? (For example, Marbod is dressing differently and has had his hair cut; Cara's father has a new role now.)

If you have time …

Ask children for their views on the title. Is it a good one? Why do they think the author chose this title?

Summing up

Ask children how the author gives us information about Cara. *(Through what she says and how she says it; what she does; how she reacts.)*

Next steps: Independent follow-up

Ask the children to write a short character sketch for Cara or Marbod to show the kind of person they are. Remind them that they must use evidence from the story to back up what they say.

Ubble in Trouble
by Douglas Hill

Year 4 Term 2 Stories of imagined worlds/science fiction

Teaching objectives

◆ Y4T2 T1 how writers create imaginary worlds (both sessions)

◆ Y4T2 T3 compare and contrast settings across a range of stories (both sessions)

◆ Y4T2 T10 develop the use of settings in own writing (Session 2)

NC level 2A

In session 1 We are going to:
- look at the setting of the story and talk about how the sci-fi part is introduced.

In session 2 We are going to:
- look closely at how well-chosen phrases help to show emotion
- compare settings.

Quick check
Things to note about this story:
- Sci-fi element in the real world
- Changes in emotions of character
- Link between beginning and end

Session 1: Reading the text

Story introduction

Explain the purpose of the session: *'We are going to read a story and find out how a writer links science fiction with the real world we live in.'*

Read the opening to the children (to 'a bit smaller than a football'). Ask the children what they think the story will be about. How do we know the object is not a football? *(It's strange, and a bit smaller than a football.)*

Strategy check

Remind the children to pay attention to commas when reading aloud. (Notice especially 'He stopped, staring' – page 22.) Model reading, if necessary.

Remind children to break down unfamiliar words into syllables.

Independent reading

If you wish to check children's reading aloud, ask them to take turns and read aloud as far as 'He raced off, towards home, to gather what he needed.' Alternatively, they could each read this passage silently.

Pause

Make a list of genre clues which tell the reader first that something odd is happening and then that an alien has arrived. *(For example, ball moves by itself, it disappears, description of Ubble, mention of spaceship, invisible spaceship.)*

Discuss the fact that these aspects of the story are woven into the realistic setting. Ask the children to reread the beginning and describe where the story starts. Notice the very detailed description of trees and long grass.

Ask the children what they think Toby is going to collect from home. What would they bring to help Ubble?

Ask the children to read to the end or, alternatively, continue to read aloud as a group.

Returning and responding to the text

What did the children think of Toby's solution?

Discuss the end of the story. Did they like it? Focus the children on the effective link between the beginning and the end by asking them to reread the first three sentences and then the very end. *(Can the children comment that the story starts with Toby being told he is useless at football? The adventure begins because he kicks something and then has to find a clever way of getting into a small space – rather like a goal! The last sentence links the kicking idea to the start of the story.)*

Before the next session

Ask the children to focus very carefully on the description of the setting at the start of the story and of Ubble's appearance.

They could draw, colour and label a picture of Ubble which shows where he was lying before Toby kicked him.

Session 2: Going deeper

Story introduction – recap

Ask the children to role-play Toby telling Ralph what happened.

Independent reading

Explain that authors often use carefully chosen words to show the emotions of their characters. Ask the children to reread the story and note down in their reading journal any words and phrases that tell them how Toby is feeling.

Returning and responding to the text

Share your own response to particular words and phrases and discuss with the children in order to act as a model. *(For example, stamped angrily away.)*

Discuss the children's ideas. Make a list of Toby's feelings and emotions through the story. *(Anger – surprise – nervousness – fear – no longer scared / interested – apologetic – pleased with himself – happy)*

Make sure the children understand that it is the careful choice of words which helps the reader know how Toby is feeling. Point out that the author does not always 'tell' us. We have to work it out.

Ask the children to reread the passage which is annotated and practise expressive reading to show Toby's changing feelings.

Shows Toby is still cross with his brother when he kicks the ball. He's not thinking about the ball.

Shows surprise. Toby cannot believe what he is seeing.

Adverb tells us how he feels. Very effective because it is at the start of the sentence. Focuses us on Toby's feelings. Rest of the paragraph – short sentences which show his fear.

Shows he cannot believe what he is seeing.

> "I'm as good as any of Ralph's lot," he <u>muttered</u>.
>
> Then he <u>stopped, staring</u>. The ball had come to rest in some taller grass, deeper among the trees. But somehow it had started moving again, as if by itself, further into the grass.
>
> And by the time Toby had <u>blinked several times</u> and looked again, the ball had disappeared.
>
> "I'm seeing things," he said to himself.
>
> <u>Nervously</u> he moved forward, still staring at the spot where the ball had been. Then he stopped again. He could hear a sound like someone crying, nearby. But he couldn't hear anyone.
>
> "Who is that?" he called. "Where are you?"
>
> "It's me," said a small voice. "I'm here."
>
> Toby took another step – and <u>froze, eyes wide</u>.

24

If you have time …

Read the higher ability level story *Monsters* to the children. Discuss the difference in the setting.

Summing up

Ask the children what they have learned about the sci-fi genre *(for example, that it includes well-described detail which is very different from the real world)* and how a writer helps the reader understand a character's emotions. *(By using well chosen words and phrases and by showing, not telling the reader what is happening.)*

Next steps: Independent follow-up

Ask the children to think about what Ubble's planet might be like, and describe it in two or three sentences.

Monsters
by Douglas Hill

Year 4 Term 2 Stories of imagined worlds/science fiction

Teaching objectives

◆ Y4T2 T1 how writers create imaginary worlds (both sessions)

◆ Y4T2 T3 compare and contrast settings across a range of stories (both sessions)

◆ Y4T2 T4 understand how expressive and descriptive language can, for example, create emotions and arouse expectations (Session 2)

◆ Y4T2 T10 develop the use of settings in own writing (Session 2)

NC level 3B – 3A

In session 1 We are going to:
◆ look at clues to the genre of the story
◆ discuss the feelings of characters
◆ compare the beginning and end of the story.

In session 2 We are going to:
◆ discuss expressive language in more detail
◆ compare settings.

Quick check
Things to note about this story:
◆ How setting is described
◆ Use of language to arouse expectations and show feelings
◆ Structure – link between beginning and end

Session 1: Reading the text

Story introduction

Explain the purpose of the session: *'We are going to read a story and find out how a writer creates an imaginary world and shows how the characters feel. We are also going to look for clues about what kind of story this is, and compare the beginning and end of the story.'*

Strategy check

Remind children that if they come across any unfamiliar words as they read, they should try to work out the meaning from the context but always note them down to check later.

Remind children to break down unfamiliar words into syllables.

Independent reading

Ask the children to read to ' "Certainly not you two" ' (page 30). Tell them to note in their reading journals any genre clues. Tell them that you will want to hear their ideas about what will happen next.

Pause

Collect the genre clues from the children. (*For example, use of words related to spaceships, descriptions of creatures, odd colours and shapes.*)

Briefly discuss their immediate response and their predictions. Look back at the first sentence as a reminder that Jorry wants to go out.

Ask the children to read on and respond to the ending.

Returning and responding to the text

Share thoughts about the ending. Ask the children whether they guessed what the 'monsters' were. If so, when? What was the clue in the text?

Point out the link between the first and the last sentence. Ask the children why they think the author started in that way and not with the paragraph starting 'Jorry and Corry were nine year old twins.' (*Beginning raises immediate interest – monsters in story. The twins are annoyed and want to go out – so they probably will!*)

Ask the children to look for evidence of how the twins' emotions change through the story *(annoyed/bored – nervous – excited – pleased with themselves)*. Talk about the fact that characters respond to events and so often you will see a change in the way someone feels or behaves during the course of the story.

Before the next session

Ask the children to reread the story and write Jorry's diary entry for that evening.

Session 2: Going deeper

Story introduction – recap

Ask the children to share some of the diary entries and use these to retell the story.

Independent reading

Remind the children that last session they looked for genre clues. Explain that a detailed description not only helps the reader to picture the imagined world but also helps him or her anticipate events.

Ask the children to read the story again and note down one or two interesting descriptions. They should also make brief notes about how these descriptions make them feel, and what they learn about the world of the story from the descriptions.

Returning and responding to the text

Share responses to the description. *(For example, the description of the monsters at the beginning of the story is a scary one and it makes the reader wonder what the monsters might do if they meet the humans.)*

Point out that the imagined world has got lots of similarities to the real world. The author has changed just a few details in order to make it very strange.

like the real Earth →

> When they reached the planet, they landed in a pleasant valley – sunlit and open, with blueish turf, purple bushes and spindly pink trees.
>
> In the pale light of two moons, they gazed around – at the thick turf, a bush with triangular leaves, a tree's feathery branches where a breeze sighed.

— different

If you have time …

Read the lower ability story *Ubble in Trouble* to the children. Discuss the differences in the setting. *(It's set on Earth with the sci-fi aspects coming through because of the visit from Ubble who is an alien.)*

Summing up

Ask the children to think about the descriptive language in the story. What three purposes does it have? *(It sets the scene in an imagined world, it conveys characters' emotions, and it arouses expectations in the reader.)*

Next steps: Independent follow-up

Remind the children that the planet the children visit is similar to Earth but there are strange differences.

Ask them to imagine that the twins had decided to explore. The children should describe what the twins might see in a short paragraph. They could start like this:

The twins decided to explore.

Food for Thought
by Michael Pryor

Year 4 Term 2 Fantasy adventures

Teaching objectives

◆ Y4T2 T1 how writers create imaginary worlds (both sessions)

◆ Y4T2 T3 compare and contrast settings (both sessions)

◆ Y4T2 T4 understand how expressive and descriptive language can, for example, create emotions and arouse expectations (Session 2)

◆ Y4T2 T13 write own examples of descriptive and expressive language based on those read (Session 2)

NC level 2A

In session 1 We are going to:
- think about how we know this is a fantasy story
- talk about the setting
- discuss what is funny in this story.

In session 2 We are going to:
- discuss expressive language in more detail
- role-play to explore what might happen next in the story.

Quick check
Things to note about this story:
- Real world setting – fantasy elements when monster arrives
- Use of expressive language to create mood
- Humour in story

Session 1: Reading the text

Story introduction

Explain the purpose of the session: *'We are going to read a story and find out how a writer uses some of the features of a fantasy story. We will also talk about the setting and humour in the story.'*

Read the first sentence aloud. Ask the children if they like it as the start of a story, and if so, why. *(For example, the opening grabs the reader's attention, and the choice of words suggests this is going to be a funny story.)*

Strategy check

Remind the children to pay attention to commas when reading aloud. (Model this, if necessary.)

Remind children to break down unfamiliar words into syllables.

Independent reading

Ask the children to read aloud around the group to the point just before the riddle game starts (page 35). Focus on expressive reading to show the feelings of Sam and the monster and to make the most of the humour. *(For example: "'I'm afraid so," said the monster. "Orders are orders, after all. So, let's get it over with, shall we?"')*

Explain the meaning of 'Co. Ltd' when the children read that section.

Pause

Ask the children to spot evidence which shows us that the story is set in the real world. *(For example, the setting – Sam's house.)* Discuss the fact that there is no detail. The reader can, therefore, imagine a house or room that he or she knows.

Ask the children how the writer shows this is a fantasy story. *(A monster comes to the door; wants to play a riddle game; may eat Sam.)*

Briefly discuss the children's predictions.

Ask the children to read to the end of the story, either independently or in pairs. Ensure that they understand the meanings of 'official representative' and 'entitled'.

Returning and responding to the text

Were their predictions right? Introduce the idea of a 'twist' in the plot – something unexpected happens.

Ask the children if they thought the story was funny. Encourage them to share evidence from the text. (They might discuss elements of the riddle game scene or the unexpected but funny last line.)

Before the next session

Ask the children to reread the story ready to retell it in their own words next session.

They could also draw and label a picture of the monster.

Session 2: Going deeper

Story introduction – recap

Ask the children to retell the story around the group, indicating when each child should start and stop.

Target careful listening and clear speaking without repetitions.

Independent reading

Explain to the children that fantasy stories need descriptive language which helps the reader imagine the fantasy part.

Ask the children to read the story again and note down a few good examples of descriptive words and phrases that help the reader imagine. They should also note down briefly how the descriptions make them feel, and what they learn about the world of the story from the descriptions.

Returning and responding to the text

Share responses to the description. Encourage the children to comment on the effect the description has on them as readers.

Three well-chosen adjectives to describe the teeth. Make the monster sound very scary.

> Sam's stomach felt <u>as if a dozen butterflies were wrestling inside it</u>, because when the monster opened its mouth, Sam saw the teeth. They were <u>long</u>, <u>sharp</u> and <u>well used</u>.

Simile – gives reader the feeling Sam is really worried – but doesn't know what about yet.

Explore what the children think might happen after the end of the story, through a 'forum theatre'. Two children take the parts of Sam Greeble and the monster. The others, and the teacher, 'direct' the scene. The 'directors' should discuss what might happen, and then tell the actors what they would like them to do. The actors should act out the scene based on the directors' instructions. They can either make up their own dialogue, or perform the scene as a mime.

If you have time …

Talk about the fact that some fantasy stories are set in the real world (like this one) and others are set in an imaginary world. Ask the children to talk about which they prefer and why. Encourage them to refer to stories they have read.

Summing up

Ask the children to think about the descriptive language in the story. Why is it important? *(It sets the scene and creates the mood. It also conveys the characters' emotions and sets up expectations for the reader.)*

Next steps: Independent follow-up

The children could write the start of the scene that they have improvised, including the monster knocking on Sam Greeble's door, and showing what happens when Sam opens it.

The children must include some more detail of:

◆ the real world
◆ the monster.

Alternatively, children could use the photocopiable writing frame on page 55 to help them write a story with a similar structure to *Food for Thought*.

The Boy Who Made Things Up
by Margaret Mahy

• •

Year 4 Term 2 Fantasy adventures

Teaching objectives

◆ Y4T2 T1 how writers create imaginary worlds (both sessions)

◆ Y4T2 T3 compare and contrast settings (both sessions)

◆ Y4T2 T4 understand how expressive and descriptive language can, for example, create emotions and arouse expectations (Session 2)

◆ Y4T2 T13 write own examples of descriptive and expressive language based on those read (Session 2)

NC level 3B – 3A

• •

In session 1 We are going to:
◆ look at how we know this is a fantasy story
◆ talk about the setting.

In session 2 We are going to:
◆ discuss expressive language in more detail.

Quick check
Things to note about this story:
◆ Real world setting – fantasy elements as boy 'makes things up'
◆ Use of expressive language to create mood, humour
◆ How father is affected

Session 1: Reading the text

Story introduction

Explain the purpose of the session: *'We are going to read a story and find out how a writer uses some of the features of a fantasy story. We will also talk about the setting.'*

Strategy check

Remind children that if they come across any unfamiliar words as they read, they should try to work out the meaning from the context but always note them down to check later.

Remind children to break down unfamiliar words into syllables.

Independent reading

Ask the children to read to ' "Can't you understand how things work yet?" Michael cried despairingly. "We make something up! Look!" ' (page 44).

Ask them to note in their reading journals any genre clues. Tell them that you will also want to hear their ideas about what happened next.

Pause

Collect the genre clues from the children. *(For example, when the boy 'makes something up' it becomes reality – this could only happen in a fantasy story!)*

Briefly discuss their immediate response and their predictions about the end of the story.

Ask the children to read on and respond to the ending.

Returning and responding to the text

Share thoughts about the ending. Ask the children if any of them thought that Michael's dad would change as a result of the walk. Why, or why not?

Discuss the setting. This is not a 'fantasy land'. The story is set in the real world. Michael's make-believe becomes real – this is what creates the fantasy.

Ask the children to find evidence that Michael has done this sort of thing before. *(At the end of the first and third paragraphs, mother's reaction at end of story.)*

Ask the children if the events of the story really happened. What is the evidence that they did *(for example, sand in shoes, sunburn)*?

Discuss the reasons why the author included this evidence (shows that the events were not just in Michael's mind, makes the reader think about the imagination as a powerful tool).

Before the next session

Ask the children to reread the story and draw a 'story map' to show the walk. They should carefully draw and label the things that Michael made up.

Session 2: Going deeper

Story introduction – recap

The children could use the detail in their story maps to retell the story around the group.

Independent reading

Remind the children that last session they looked for genre clues. Explain that a detailed description not only helps the reader to picture the fantasy part of the story but also makes the reader react in certain ways.

Ask the children to read the story again and note down a few examples of descriptive language which they find effective. (It may be a good idea to give different members of the group different sections to reread, in order to focus more closely on the language.)

Returning and responding to the text

Share responses to the description. *(For example: the description of the path makes the reader feel there will be something unusual or exciting at the end; the section when they first see the sea and sand gives a calm, quiet impression; the section about the ice-cream seller is funny.)*

Adjectives

Similes

> The boy and his father swam out to the islands without getting in the least bit tired. The water was <u>warm</u>, yet <u>tingling</u>, and <u>as clear as green grass</u>. Shoals of <u>bright</u> fish, as <u>small and shiny as needles</u>, followed them and <u>tickled</u> their feet. <u>Down, down, far down</u> under the water, the sand <u>shone silver</u> with <u>black</u> fish all over it, <u>like a night sky pulled inside out</u>. The boy and his father swam in and out among the islands. Waves <u>burst</u> on the rocks around them and <u>rainbows in the spray curled</u> over their heads.

Well-chosen and powerful verbs.

Effective repetition – links back to fact water is so clear.

Look at other similes and ask the children how they help to build up a picture.

If you have time …

Examine the thoughts and feelings of Michael's father at different points of the story by putting him in the hot-seat. Focus on the change in him and the suggestion that he enjoyed making things up and is going to be doing more of it in the future!

Summing up

Ask the children to think about the descriptive language in the story.

What two main purposes does it have? *(It sets the scene in Michael's made-up world and helps to create the carefree fantasy mood.)*

Next steps: Independent follow-up

The children could imagine that Michael and his father explore something else *(for example, rock pools, a cave)* or meet someone else *(Punch and Judy man, a boy flying a kite)*.

They should write three or four sentences to describe the scene using:

◆ adjectives
◆ powerful verbs
◆ similes.

Alternatively, the children could write a few sentences to describe a favourite daydream coming true.

How to Win at Football
by Rachel Anderson

Year 4 Term 3 Issues and dilemmas

Teaching objectives

- ◆ Y4T3 T1 identify and discuss social, cultural and moral issues in stories (both sessions)
- • Y4T3 T3 understand how paragraphs are used to collect, order and build up ideas (Session 1)
- • Y4T3 T11 write a story about a dilemma (Session 2)

NC level 3C

In session 1 We are going to:
- ◆ look at how the plot moves along
- ◆ discuss how the paragraphs organise the detail of the story.

In session 2 We are going to:
- ◆ discuss how different people behave in the story
- ◆ think about what the story is about.

Quick check
Things to note about this story:
- ◆ Development of the plot – use of paragraphing to build up detail
- ◆ Issue of involving a disabled person

Note for teacher

This story explores the issues involved in the inclusion of a child with learning difficulties in school life. Sensitive handling of the story will be needed, particularly if there are children with learning difficulties in the class.

Session 1: Reading the text

Story introduction

Explain the purpose of the session: *'We are going to read a story and look carefully at the build-up of the plot in the paragraphs.'*

Read the opening paragraph and ask the children what they think the children in the story were thinking when Mrs Khan said that the new boy was very special.

Strategy check

Remind the children to pay attention to commas when reading aloud, and to break down unfamiliar words into syllables.

Revise silent letters, if needed (*wriggled, wrecked*).

Skimming where summarising the plot.

Independent reading

If you wish to check children's reading aloud, ask them to take turns and read aloud as far as 'I think he understood' (page 50). Alternatively, they could each read this passage silently.

As they read, they should notice examples of things that Danny did which annoyed other children. *(For example, he shouted and wriggled in class, grabbed the football. In other words his behaviour was different from everyone else's.)*

Pause

Ask the children what they think will happen next. What do they think Wayne and the other children will say when they see Danny with the rattle?

Ask the children to read to the end of the story, either independently or aloud in the group.

Returning and responding to the text

Were the children's predictions right? Did they like the ending? Help the children to justify their opinions with reference to the text.

Work with the children to sum up the different sections of the story in a few words. *(For example, Danny arrives – problems at school; the narrator decides to help; idea of rattle; the match; ending – things are better.)* Encourage the children to skim down the sections to summarise them, rather than reading every word.

Point out to the children that there are often several paragraphs within a section of the plot, and each paragraph adds further details. Ask the children to look at the first five paragraphs and discuss what each one is about. *(For example: new boy coming; Danny's problems; where he sits; who helps him; how he annoys people.)*

Before the next session

Ask the children to reread the story. They could then draw two 'think bubbles' and write inside them (a) one thing Danny might have been thinking during the school day; (b) something he might have been thinking after the match on Friday.

Session 2: Going deeper

Story introduction – recap

Ask the children to retell the story by describing what they think Danny's thoughts might be at different points of the story. Prompt the children to move on by telling them that the scene has changed.

Independent reading

Explain that short stories often deal with how people get along together. Ask the children to reread the story and look for any changes that happen in the way the different characters get along.

Returning and responding to the text

Share the children's ideas. Lead them in a discussion about helping people with disabilities – how they might feel; what they want; how they can be helped.

Ask the children to discuss what might have happened if Wayne had been sitting next to Danny rather than the boy who tells the story. Would things have been different? Why did the boy understand? Where had he got his idea for help from? Is it hard to understand people who are different?

The boy's first impression – that Danny is a nuisance. He repeats Wayne's view to justify it.

Dad gives a different opinion. Talks about Grandad wanting to join in.

On the way home, I told my dad about the new boy always spoiling our fun. Dad said, "I dare say he's only trying to be friendly."

"Wayne says he does it on purpose to annoy us."

Dad said, "Or perhaps he's trying to say he wants to join in, even if he can't play? D'you remember how much your grandad used to enjoy the football, by cheering on his team?"

"Sort of," I said. I could just about remember Grandad sitting close up to the telly and waving a special wooden rattle.

When I told Wayne what my dad had said about the new boy, Wayne said, "Don't be daft! How could Danny join in? He doesn't understand the first thing about sport, let alone teamwork."

Wayne's view has not changed.

I said, "I'll find a way."

"Yeah yeah yeah," said Wayne. I knew he didn't believe me.

The boy is now determined to help – not copying Wayne's comments any more.

40

Look at the very end of the story and find the previous reference to trainers (paragraph 2). Ask the children what they thought the boy meant at the beginning of the story. *(For example, that Danny couldn't do up his trainers.)* What does the end suggest? *(That he could do them up – but put other people's on!)*

If you have time …

Hot-seat Wayne to find out about his attitude to Danny before and after the football match.

Summing up

Ask the children who was helped by the boy's idea *(Everyone)*. Does the story have a message?

Remind the children that the detail in the story is built up through the paragraphs.

Next steps: Independent follow-up

Children could plan a story about someone who is being unfairly treated for a different reason, and how someone helps out.

Children could use the photocopiable writing frame on page 55 to help with this.

Doppelganger.com
by Jan-Andrew Henderson

Year 4 Term 3 Issues and dilemmas

Teaching objectives

◆ Y4T3 T1 identify and discuss social, cultural and moral issues in stories (both sessions)

◆ Y4T3 T3 understand how paragraphs are used to collect, order and build up ideas (Session 1)

◆ Y4T3 T11 write a story about a dilemma (Session 2)

NC level 3A

In session 1 We are going to:
• look at how the plot moves along
• discuss how the paragraphs organise the detail of the story.

In session 2 We are going to:
• discuss how the author shows William is afraid
• think about what the story is about.

Quick check

Things to note about this story:

◆ Development of the plot – use of paragraphing to build up detail

◆ Issue of potential dangers of the internet

◆ An ending that suggests there is more to come

Session 1: Reading the text

Story introduction

Explain the purpose of the session: *'We are going to read a story and look carefully at the build up of the plot in the paragraphs.'*

Read the first two paragraphs and ask the children what they think the story is going to be about.

Strategy check

Note: do not deal in advance with the meaning of the word 'doppelganger'. Discuss the strategies for working out meaning by reading on and from the context. The children will gain more insight into the story if they don't understand what a doppelganger is to begin with, because William does not understand the meaning at first.

Remind children to break down unfamiliar words into syllables.

Independent reading

Ask the children to read independently to 'There was a ping from my PC and I glanced over to it' (page 54).

As they read, ask them to note any words related to computers in their reading journals. Tell them that when they have finished the section, you will also want to hear their ideas about what happened next.

Pause

Collect the words related to computers. *(For example, web, website, surfing the net, scan, send, pop-up box, PC.)*

Briefly discuss children's immediate responses and predictions. Now that they know what a doppelganger is, what do they think has happened? How will the story end?

Ask the children to read to the end.

Returning and responding to the text

Were the children's predictions right? Did they like the ending? Why, or why not? Encourage children to explain their responses by reference to the text.

Discuss the change of tense at the end. Why is the story written like that? *(For example, to underline William's worry – now.)* Why are the last two words repeated? *(Perhaps to suggest that something is going to happen?)*

Work with the children to summarise the different sections of the story. Encourage them to skim down the sections to find the main points. *(For example, surfing the net, filling in form, waiting – using dictionary, doppelganger appears, more waiting …)*

Point out to the children that there are often several paragraphs within a section of the plot in order to add detail. *(For example, in the second section of the story – William enters site, fills in details, scans picture, information appears, he waits.)*

Before the next session

Ask the children to reread the story. They could then draw three 'think bubbles' and write inside them what William might be thinking:

◆ at the beginning of the story
◆ as he fills out the questionnaire
◆ at the end.

Session 2: Going deeper

Story introduction – recap

Ask the children to retell the story around the group, using the think bubbles as prompts (see 'Before the next section', page 43).

Independent reading

Explain that short stories often deal with important issues that people need to think about. Ask the children to reread the story and look for any message that they think it might have for the reader.

Returning and responding to the text

Share the children's ideas. Lead them in a discussion about the use of the internet. Is everything on the internet safe? Is it all right to fill in forms like that? What should William have done first? Focus children on the section that starts, 'It's a website. Things on the web can't hurt you.'

Discuss how the writer uses words carefully to show how what has happened has really scared the boy.

Deliberate repetition and use of italics to underline surprise.

> I was on the computer screen. A picture of me. *I was on the computer screen.*
>
> I got up from the bed and walked slowly across the room. The image on the PC was identical to me in every way, all except for the <u>eyes</u>. The <u>eyes were empty and flat as paint</u>.
>
> <u>Suddenly</u> the boy on the screen turned his head and smiled at me. My heart lurched. <u>Hardly breathing</u>, I reached slowly for the mouse. <u>Still smiling</u>, his image followed the movement of my hand, then looked up at me and slowly shook its head.

Adverb starter – to suggest something is about to happen.

Short sentence gives contrast. Emphasises fear. Powerful verb.

Repetition of 'eyes' followed by a powerful and scary description.

'Hardly breathing' is put first in the sentence to underline the boy's feelings and fear. The next sentence mirrors the construction – 'still smiling' – related to the doppelganger.

The children could role-play in twos what might happen after the end of the story.

If you have time …

Discuss whether William will learn his lesson. Point out that the way the story is written (everything is normal at first, then things become stranger and stranger, and William becomes more and more afraid) shows that apparently small steps can lead to very important or unpleasant consequences.

Summing up

Remind the children about the sections of the story and how it built up to a very effective end which makes the reader imagine what might happen next. What aspects of the way this story is written do children feel they would want to use in their own writing? *(For example, using paragraphs to build up detail; showing the action from the point of view of the main character so the reader feels the character's emotions; using an open ending to make the reader think.)*

Next steps: Independent follow-up

Write the next scene of the story using the role-play to help with ideas.

Alternatively, children could use the photocopiable writing frame on page 56 to help them write a story with a similar structure to *Doppelganger.com*.

The Rock

by Julie Till

Year 4 Term 3 Stories from other cultures (Oman)

Teaching objectives

- Y4T3 T1 identify and discuss social, cultural and moral issues in stories (both sessions)
- Y4T3 T2 read stories from other cultures; focus on, for example, differences in place, time, customs, relationships (both sessions)
- Y4T3 T12 write an alternate ending for a known story (Session 2)

NC level 3C

In session 1 We are going to:
- think about how we know that the story is set in another country
- discuss the build-up of the plot.

In session 2 We are going to:
- discuss what the story tells us about the way people live in different places.

Quick check

Things to note about this story:
- Development of the plot – meaning of ending
- Evidence of setting and culture
- Issues – bravery, role of girls

Session 1: Reading the text

Story introduction

Explain the purpose of the session: *'We are going to read a story, look carefully at how we know it is set in another country and talk about the plot.'*

Read the opening section. Use an atlas, if necessary, to ensure that the children know the location of Oman.

Strategy check

Remind the children to pay attention to commas when reading aloud. If needed, model how to read a longer sentence aloud and pay attention to the punctuation.

Remind children to break down unfamiliar words into syllables.

Independent reading

If you wish to check children's reading aloud, ask them to take turns and read aloud as far as 'Wave after wave slapped against the rock, as if the sea wanted him back' (page 58). Alternatively, ask them each to read this passage silently.

Tell the children that when they have read the passage you will ask them for their predictions about what may happen next.

Pause

Briefly ask the children for their responses and predictions. What do they think Zeinab will do? Discuss the dilemma which is going through her mind. How do the children think the story will end?

Ask the children to read to the end of the story, either independently or aloud in the group.

Returning and responding to the text

Were the children's predictions right? Did they like the ending?

Ask the children to scan the text and note down evidence about the setting of the story. What are the differences between Zeinab's way of life and the children's? (*For example, flat roof of the house; staircase on the outside of the house; old motor boat – so no lifeboat; desert; Zeinab was used to extra weight of her clothes in the water – suggests she didn't normally wear a swimming costume in the sea.*)

Look at further detail about the setting: the author's description of the rough sea and the choice of powerful verbs (*spat, slapped, crashed*) to create a sense of danger.

Work with the children to summarise the different sections of the story. (*For example, Zeinab not allowed to fish; boy disappears; Zeinab spots him; swims out; saves him; goes fishing the next Friday.*) Encourage the children to skim down the sections to give them headings rather than read every word.

Before the next session

Ask the children to reread the story. They could then write down what they think Zeinab's brothers might have said when she got out of the water.

Session 2: Going deeper

Story introduction – recap

Ask the children to retell the story in the form of an interview which happened after the rescue. They could play different characters, for example: interviewer, Zeinab, woman on the beach, the boy, Zeinab's brother(s). The interviewer could start by asking Zeinab what she was doing earlier in the day.

Independent reading

Explain that short stories that are set in other countries give us a glimpse of the way of life and the culture of a different place.

Ask the children to reread the story and look for evidence about the kind of life Zeinab leads.

Returning and responding to the text

Share the children's ideas. What evidence is there about Zeinab's role in the family and the expectations her relatives have for her?

Compare the beginning and the end of the story. Discuss the change in Zeinab's brothers' attitude that is implied and the reason for it.

Implied attitude to girls in Oman.

Acceptance by Zeinab without any arguing.

> Zeinab's brothers went fishing every Friday. Zeinab wanted to go with them. She followed them to the beach and watched her brothers as they prepared the boat.
>
> "Go home, Zeinab. You're too young."
>
> "Go home, Zeinab. It's too dangerous for you."
>
> Disappointed, Zeinab turned around and made her way back home.
>
> That afternoon, Zeinab and her mother were hanging out the washing on the flat roof of their house when they heard a loud wailing and shouting.
>
> ★ ★ ★
>
> The following Friday Zeinab went fishing with her brothers.

Zeinab has to help her mother.

Brothers realize what she can do. Perhaps they also want to reward her for her bravery.

Ask the children to think about what Zeinab did in relation to this attitude to girls. Do they think she was brave? Ask the children to look for evidence about whether she was confident or not. (*She lied about swimming to the rock to make the boy feel happier – but she was worried.*) How would the children have felt in Zeinab's position? Some aspects of

Zeinab's life may be different from the children's own lives – what are the similarities between Zeinab and the children? *(For example, wanting to help someone in distress; responding to the need for help; being brave when necessary. . .)*

If you have time …

Look again at the section from 'It was safer to go and get help' to 'I have to turn back before the waves take me' (page 58). Ask the children what is going on. Do they realise that the passage contains Zeinab's thoughts?

Summing up

Ask the children for two ways in which the author has made the setting in Oman vivid for the reader. (*By including detail about the area and evidence of people's way of life and attitudes.*)

Next steps: Independent follow-up

Ask the children to plan a further chapter for the story, when Zeinab goes out with her brothers the following Friday.

Alternatively, children could use the photocopiable writing frame on page 56 to help them write a story with a similar structure to *The Rock*.

Zanzibar Treasures

by Adam Guillain

Year 4 Term 3 Stories from other cultures (Zanzibar)

Teaching objectives

- ◆ Y4T3 T1 identify and discuss social, cultural and moral issues in stories (both sessions)
- ◆ Y4T3 T2 read stories from other cultures; focus on, for example, differences in place, time, customs, relationships (both sessions)
- ◆ Y4T3 T12 write an alternative ending for a known story (session 2)

NC level 3A

In session 1 We are going to:
- ◆ think about the way the author gives us a lot of detail about the place, customs and way of life.

In session 2 We are going to:
- ◆ discuss the messages that the story gives to the reader.

Quick check

Things to note about this story:
- ◆ Evidence of setting, religion and culture
- ◆ Issues – what is treasure?
- ◆ Importance of imagination and perseverance

Session 1: Reading the text

Story introduction

Explain the purpose of the session: *'We are going to read a story and look at how the author tells us about the customs and way of life in another country.'*

Read the opening paragraph. Ask the children for evidence that the story is set in another country. *(For example, tropical current; spices; no-one Hamadi knew owned a shoe; dala dala; polishing tourists' shoes; buying sack of maize flour.)*

Ask the children what they think the story will be about.

Use an atlas, if necessary, to ensure that the children know the location of Zanzibar.

Strategy check

Remind children that if they come across any unfamiliar words as they read, they should try to work out the meaning from the context but always note them down to check later.

Ask the children what they think a 'dala dala' might be. The context suggests it is a form of transport – in fact it is a local bus.

Remind children to break down unfamiliar words into syllables.

Independent reading

Ask the children to read independently to: 'Disappointed, they dropped it into the bag and headed for home' (page 63).
As they read, the children should jot down more evidence of life and customs in Zanzibar.

Pause

Briefly ask the children for their responses and predictions. What do they think will happen next?

Ask the children to read to the end of the story.

Returning and responding to the text

Were the children's predictions right? Did they like the ending? Did they think that a use would be found for the treasure or did they think the girls would go back and find 'real treasure'?

Collect evidence about the customs and way of life in Zanzibar. In addition, notice the references to Islam. *(Muezzin, mosque, madrassa, Koran, Islamic gown and hat.)*

Discuss the fact that the evidence of the setting in a different country is included throughout the story and not just at the beginning. *(For example, there is mention of school, religion, life at home, clothes, food etc. throughout.)* This gives the reader a real sense of the place.

Before the next session

Ask the children to reread the story and be ready to retell it during the next session.

Session 2: Going deeper

Story introduction – recap

Ask one of the children to start to retell the story. At a signal, the next member of the group should take over. Ask the children to concentrate on listening hard to ensure there is no repetition.

Independent reading

Explain that short stories often tell us a lot about different people's attitudes to ordinary events and this means they sometimes make us think about the way we behave ourselves.

Ask the children to reread the story and note down anything they think the girls learned from the day at the beach.

Returning and responding to the text

Role-play the section of the story when the girls find the objects and then the following day at home. Two children should play the parts of Kulsum and Samira. 'Freeze frame' the role-play at certain points and ask the other children to question the 'girls'. For example, the children might ask about what they are thinking, why they haven't gone home already, why they are hunting for 'treasure', what they think about what has been done with the 'rubbish' they found, and so on.

Move into a whole-group discussion about what this has shown about the girls and others in their family. *(For example, they are excited when they talk about the treasure; they show perseverance – they keep going, even though they are disappointed; their father uses his imagination to see different uses for the objects.)*

Discuss what actually happened to the objects. Relate this to the title of the story and to the ending. What were the girls looking for? What did they find?

Evidence of story set in another country – food they are eating.

> "I think we should go <u>treasure hunting</u> tomorrow," suggested <u>Samira</u> as they washed their hands ready to eat their <u>octopus and rice</u>. "See what other <u>riches</u> we can find.'"

Link to the start of the story and to the title.

Realisation that they have found riches – as their brother had when he found the shoe polish. What is rubbish to one person is a treasure to another.

If you have time …

Ask the children to talk about any objects that they have which might seem like rubbish to someone else but are very special to them.

Summing up

Ask the children what messages this story can give a reader. *(For example, to keep going if you want something, and the fact that you need a bit of imagination to see what some things can be used for.)*

Next steps: Independent follow-up

Ask the children to write an alternative ending by continuing the story into the next day. Do the girls go treasure hunting again? If so, what do they find?

Photocopiable Story Writing Frame

'Character' story – based on *The Grey Gander*

1. X is in charge of something, but is forgetful.

2. Disaster strikes.

3. But – X performs a good deed.

4. Y discovers what has happened.

5. X fears the worst, but Y rewards X.

(Note: X = main character.   Y = other character.)

Photocopiable Story Writing Frame

'Making friends' story – based on *My Name is Jim*

1. X and Y dislike each other.

2. Y picks on/bullies X.

3. Y is in a dangerous situation.

4. X saves/helps Y.

5. They make friends.

(Note: X = main character.   Y = other character.)

Photocopiable Story Writing Frame

'Contest' story – based on *Food for Thought*

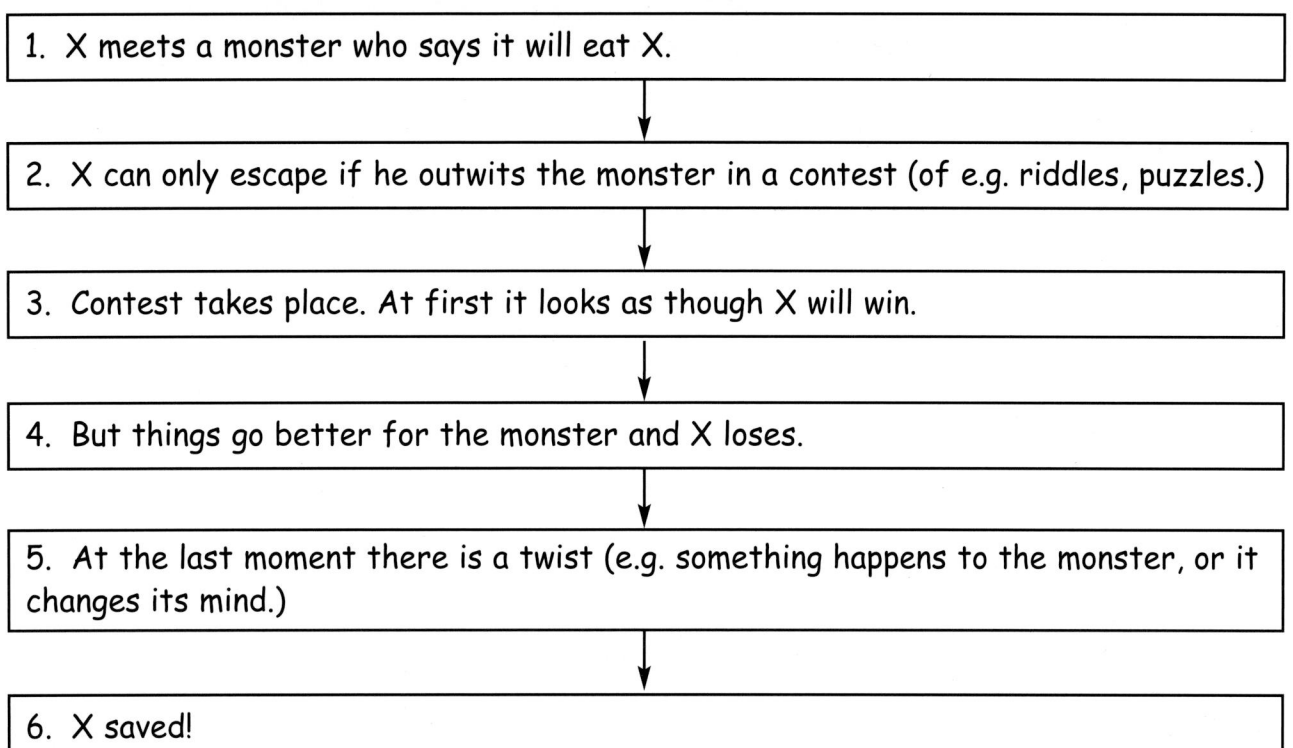

1. X meets a monster who says it will eat X.

2. X can only escape if he outwits the monster in a contest (of e.g. riddles, puzzles.)

3. Contest takes place. At first it looks as though X will win.

4. But things go better for the monster and X loses.

5. At the last moment there is a twist (e.g. something happens to the monster, or it changes its mind.)

6. X saved!

- - - - - - ✂ -

Photocopiable Story Writing Frame

'Joining In' story – based on *How to Win at Football*

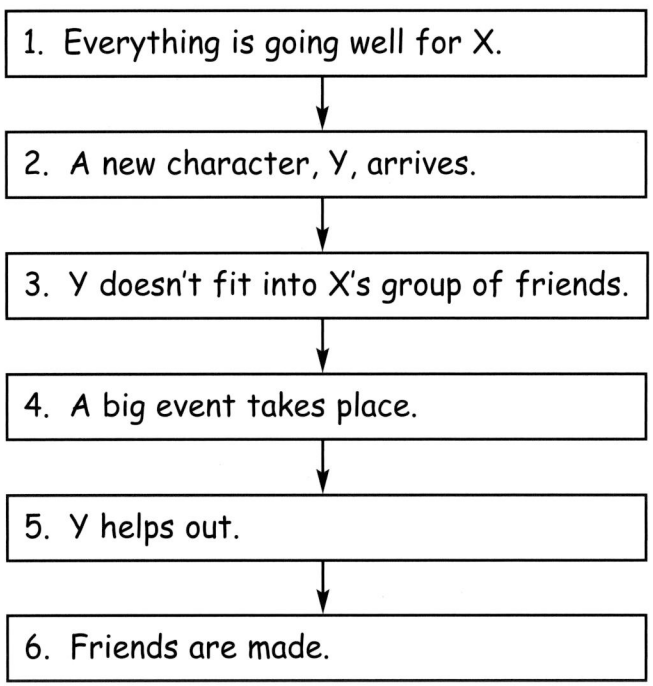

1. Everything is going well for X.

2. A new character, Y, arrives.

3. Y doesn't fit into X's group of friends.

4. A big event takes place.

5. Y helps out.

6. Friends are made.

(Note: X = main character.   Y = other character.)

Photocopiable Story Writing Frame

'Sinister creation' story – based on _Doppelganger.com_

1. X browses, e.g. a computer, books in a library.

2. X finds mysterious offer/instruction for making something.

3. X doesn't understand what the 'something' is.

4. X thinks it sounds interesting, and follows the instructions anyway.

5. Something scary happens.

6. X is frightened that he/she has made something he/she can't control.

Photocopiable Story Writing Frame

'Proving oneself' story – based on _The Rock_

1. X wants to join in activity (e.g. a sport, an outing).

2. X is told that he/she is too young/not good enough to join in.

3. Y is lost.

4. X finds Y.

5. X saves Y.

6. X allowed to join in activity.

(Note: X = main character.   Y = other character.)